CHILDREN'S MUSEUMS

by Emma Bassier

Cody Koala

An Imprint of Pop!
popbooksonline.com

abdobooks.com
Published by Pop!, a division of ABDO, PO Box 398166, Minneapolis,
Minnesota 55439. Copyright © 2020 by POP, LLC. International copyrights
reserved in all countries. No part of this book may be reproduced in any
form without written permission from the publisher. Pop!™ is a trademark
and logo of POP, LLC.

Printed in the United States of America, North Mankato, Minnesota

052019
092019

THIS BOOK CONTAINS
RECYCLED MATERIALS

Cover Photo: William S. Kuta/Alamy
Interior Photos: William S. Kuta/Alamy, 1; iStockphoto, 5 (top), 5 (bottom left),
5 (bottom right), 8, 11, 13, 16, 19 (top), 19 (bottom left), 19 (bottom right), 20;
Shutterstock Images, 7, 9, 14, 15

Editor: Meg Gaertner
Series Designer: Jake Slavik

Library of Congress Control Number: 2018964771

Publisher's Cataloging-in-Publication Data

Names: Bassier, Emma, author.
Title: Children's museums / by Emma Bassier.
Description: Minneapolis, Minnesota : Pop!, 2020 | Series: Places in my
    community | Includes online resources and index.
Identifiers: ISBN 9781532163463 (lib. bdg.) | ISBN 9781532164903 (ebook)
Subjects: LCSH: Children's museums--Juvenile literature. | Museums and
    community--Juvenile literature.
Classification: DDC 507.4--dc23

Hello! My name is

Cody Koala

Pop open this book and you'll find QR codes like this one, loaded with information, so you can learn even more!

Scan this code* and others like it while you read, or visit the website below to make this book pop.

popbooksonline.com/childrens-museums

*Scanning QR codes requires a web-enabled smart device with a QR code reader app and a camera.

Table of Contents

Museums

People go to **museums** to learn. They can look at interesting objects in museums. Children's museums are specially made for young visitors.

Watch a video here!

A Place to Explore

Children's **museums** are a place to explore. Children walk through different rooms. They use their **senses** to play and learn.

Learn more here!

One sense is sight.

Children might see tiny

things through a **microscope**.

Another sense is touch.

Children might dig for **fossils**.

They feel the sand.

Two more senses are hearing and taste. Children might play drums or hear bells ringing. They might make and taste new foods.

The Children's Museum of Indianapolis is the largest in the world.

The Five Senses

sight

smell

hearing

taste

touch

Chapter 3

Inside a Children's Museum

Inside a children's **museum** there are **exhibits**. These displays teach visitors about different topics. One could be about farms. Another could be about bubbles.

Complete an activity here!

Some exhibits are like
real life. Children can put on
costumes. They can act like
they are at a market.

Other exhibits are about the past. Children can learn about dinosaurs. They can touch **fossils**.

Some museums have classrooms. Children can go to classes about interesting topics. They might go on a walk outside. They might make art.

Kohl Children's Museum in Chicago has story time.

Chapter 4

Hands-On Learning

People learn in many different ways. Children's **museums** help children learn through their **senses**. Children get to hear, touch, and see new things.

Learn more here!

Everyone is welcome at a children's museum. Some schools take **field trips** to museums. The students play and learn.

Making Connections

Text-to-Self

Have you ever been to a children's museum? If yes, what was it like? If no, would you like to visit one? Why or why not?

Text-to-Text

Have you read other books about museums?
How are those museums similar to or different from children's museums?

Text-to-World

A children's museum is a place to explore.
Where else can people go to explore or learn?

Glossary

exhibit – a public display.

field trip – a trip students take to a place away from their school.

fossil – the remains of a plant or an animal from a long time ago.

microscope – a tool scientists use to view very small objects.

museum – a place that has many rooms and exhibits about different topics.

sense – one of the five ways that humans take in information.

Index

Online Resources

popbooksonline.com

Thanks for reading this Cody Koala book!

Scan this code* and others like it in this book, or visit the website below to make this book pop!

popbooksonline.com/childrens-museums

*Scanning QR codes requires a web-enabled smart device with a QR code reader app and a camera.